DAD JOKES FOR KIDS

400+Hilarious Dad Jokes to Make Your Family Laugh Out Loud

Cooper the Pooper

TABLE OF CONTENTS

Table of Contents 3

Introduction 4

Chapter 1: Corny One-Liners 6

Chapter 2: Hyper-Literal Jokes 70

Chapter 3: Anecdotes 86

Final Words 110

INTRODUCTION

Well hello there, fellow jokester!

I hope you are ready for some serious giggles.

Now, I would have you know that I love all sorts of jokes. Knock-knock jokes, "would you rather" jokes, and silly one-liners – they are all great.

But there is one type of joke that I love more than any other.

Yep, *dad* jokes.

I know what you are thinking – dad jokes are *lame*.

But nothing could be further from the truth.

A good dad joke will have you shaking your head at the sheer silliness of it all. It will have you cringing from the lameness. And most of all, it will have you rolling around on the ground laughing – well, once you finally get it, that is.

And guess what?

You have all my best dad jokes in the palm of your hand – and they are guaranteed to get some laughs.

I used to spend all my time laying in the sun, digging through trash, chasing cats, and playing with the local kids. But then rather than play with *me*, those kids started spending all their time glued to the screen of their phones.

How boring!

So, I came up with some ways kids like you can have fun with your friends and family. Yep, you guessed it, I started writing books. And honestly, what better way to have some fun than by sharing a couple (or a couple of hundred...) dad jokes.

If you are looking for some dad jokes to share with your best friend, have some laughs with your family, or simply have a giggle in your bedroom, then I have got you covered – because in your hand you have more than 400 of the funniest dad jokes on the planet.

But make sure you don't laugh too hard – I don't want you to break a funny bone!

01

I keep all of my dad jokes in a...
- **dad-a-base!**

02

I'm sleepy.
- **Nice to meet you, Sleepy. I'm Dad!**

03

What is a witch's favorite subject to learn in school?
- **SPELLing.**

04

How do you make a lemon drop?
- **You let it FALL.**

05

You know what is brown, hairy, and wears sunglasses?
- **A coconut on a tropical vacation.**

06

Why is it that when you look for a lost item, you find it in the last place that you look?

- **Because when you find it, you can stop looking.**

07

What did the teddy bear say at the restaurant when the waiter asked if she wanted dessert?

- **No thanks, I'm STUFFED.**

08

What has ears but can't hear anything?

- **A field of corn!**

09

What did the limestone rock shout at the geologist?

- **You better not take me for GRANITE!**

10

What kind of water cannot freeze?

- **Hot water!**

11

Knock Knock!

Who's there?

I care about.

I care about who?

- **I care about you!**

12

Why do pirates have only one eye?

- **Because the word pirate has only one I.**

13

What is red and very bad for your teeth?

- **A brick.**

14

What event do beef burgers dance at?

- **MeatBALLS.**

15

How many tickles does it take for you to make an octopus break down laughing?

- **TEN-tickles.**

16

Sometimes, I tuck my knees in toward my chest and I lean forward until I start to move.

- **That's just how I ROLL.**

17

Knock Knock!
Who's there?
Dwayne.
Dwayne who?

- **Dwayne the sink; the bathroom's full of water now.**

18

I told my friend I was going to build a bike out of only spaghetti noodles.

- **She just couldn't believe her eyes when I rode PASTA.**

19

Have you heard the story of the sandwich that could fly?

- **Never mind; it's just a load of baloney!**

20

Want to hear a joke about a stone?

- **Never mind, I can just skip it!**

21

Why did Tigger get his head stuck down a toilet bowl?

- **He was looking for Pooh!**

22

Why do ducks have flat feet?

- **To stamp out forest fires.**

And why is it that elephants also have flat feet?

- **So they can stamp out flaming ducks!**

23

Why did King Kong climb up the side of the Empire State Building?

- **Because he couldn't quite fit in the elevator.**

24

Why are mountains so funny?

• **Because they are hill-areas!**

25

What do clouds love to do when they become rich?

• **Make it RAIN.**

26

Why do ghosts make such good cheerleaders?

• **They have so much spirit in them.**

27

Knock Knock!

Who's there?

I eat mop.

I eat mop, who?

• **You said "I eat ma poo!"**

28

What's black all over when it's clean?

• **A chalkboard.**

29

What color is the wind?
Invisible.

• **No, it's BLEW.**

30

Why did the fish blush?

• **Because it caught a glimpse of the ocean's BOTTOM.**

31

What begins with an E and ends with an E, but isn't a one-letter word?

• **An envelope.**

32

What do you get when you combine a fish and an elephant?

• **Swimming trunks.**

33

Why is a river rich?

- **Because it has banks.**

34

What's the difference between a babysitter and a train?

- **One will tell you to spit out the gum, while the other will say to you, "Choo, choo, choo!"**

35

Why did the painting get arrested?

- **Because it was FRAMED!**

36

What is a cat's favorite breakfast cereal?

- **MICE Krispies.**

37

The inventor of the knock-knock joke should receive...

- **A noBEL prize.**

38

How many snowboarders does it take to successfully screw in a lightbulb?

- **50- three to die trying, one to pull it off, and 46 additional ones to say, "Man, I coulda done that!"**

39

Have you heard of that restaurant, Karma?

- **There isn't any menu, so instead of ordering food, you just get served what you deserve.**

40

Why did the witches' team lose the ball game?

- **Their bats flew away.**

41

What did the mother bullet say to the father bullet?

- **We're gonna have a BB!**

42

Who is the security outside of a Samsung store called?

- **The guardians of the Galaxy.**

43

What kinds of sandals do frogs like to wear?

- **Open-TOAD.**

44

Why did the school kids eat their homework?

- **Because their teacher said, "Don't worry, it's a piece of cake."**

45

What do computers love to eat when they're hungry?

- **MicroCHIPS.**

46

What's the main difference between a fish and a guitar?

- **While you may be able to tune a guitar, you can't TUNA fish.**

47

What's a shark's favorite sandwich to eat?

- **Peanut butter and jellyfish.**

48

What do you call it when a pig does karate kicks?

• **A pork CHOP!**

49

Why did the can crusher have to quit his job?

• **Because it was soda-pressing.**

50

What is it called when a city is powered by electricity?

• **An electri-CITY!**

51

How do trains eat?

• **They chew-chew!**

52

What is a foot long and super slippery?

• **A slipper...**

53

Why is England one of the wettest countries?

- **Because for as long as I can remember, kings and queens have been REIGNING there.**

54

Why can't Pacman use social media?

- **Because he hates being FOLLOWED.**

55

I have a fear of speed bumps, but guess what?

- **I am slowly getting OVER it.**

56

What do you call a father who fell through ice?

- **A POP-sicle.**

57

What did the police officer say to his stomach?

- **You're under a vest.**

58

What's another way to say that an Italian chef died?

- **He PASTA way.**

59

Why did the dinosaur have to cross the road?

- **Because the chicken joke hadn't been invented yet.**

60

I was admiring my ceiling today.

- **Not sure if it's the best ceiling ever, but it sure is UP there.**

61

Why does Humpty Dumpty love when autumn comes around?

- **Because Humpty Dumpty had a great fall.**

62

Why are libraries too strict?

- **They have to go by the book.**

63

What is easy to get yourself into but hard to get yourself out of?

• **Trouble.**

64

What do you call the only green musician to ever live?

• **Elvis Parsley.**

65

What is the difference between a good joke and bad timing?

• **Dogs may not be able to use MRI machines, but CATSCAN.**

66

What do porcupines say to each other when they kiss?

• **"Ouch!"**

67

What is an astronaut's favorite computer key?

• **The SPACE bar.**

68

Why did the man fall into the well?

• **Because he can't see that WELL.**

69

How do you impress a baker when you are taking their daughter on a date?

• **You bring her FLOURS.**

70

Why was six scared of seven?

• **Because seven ate nine.**

71

Why does everyone fall in love with robbers?

• **Because they steal hearts.**

72

Why do cats love computers?

• **They get to chase a mouse around!**

73 When the church found a new location,
- **it had to have an ORGAN transplant.**

74 What is another word for twins?
- **Wombmates.**

75 Which planet is the most similar to the circus?
- **Saturn, because it has three rings on it.**

76 What is it called when a hen leaves her coop?
- **An eggs-it.**

77 The Earth's rotation...
- **Makes my DAY.**

78

Although I hurt my finger chopping cheese,
- **I could have GRATER problems.**

79

Why was Dumbo the elephant so sad?
- **Because he felt irrELEPHANT.**

80

What happens to your body if you eat a bunch of spaghettiOs?
- **You have a VOWEL movement.**

81

June is over??
- **Julying.**

82

Why are chefs so scary?
- **Because they beat their eggs and whipped cream.**

83

You know what would make me feel uplifted?
- **Being able to fly.**

84

Why do tennis players prefer to buy nine rackets?
- **Because TENNIS too many.**

85

How do mountains see everything?
- **They PEAK.**

86

Why did the candle have to quit his job?
- **Because he got burnt out.**

87

How do frogs get so happy?
- **They eat everything that BUGS them.**

88 What does a dog yell when he sits on a piece of sandpaper?

• **RUFF!**

89 I would tell you a joke about chemistry,

• **but it may not get a REACTION.**

90 What is the name of the girl with one leg that is longer than the other?

• **EiLEEN.**

91 *Knock Knock!*

Who's there?
Orange.
Orange who?

• **Orange you going to give me a snack?**

92 At the disco-themed seafood party last week,

• **I pulled a MUSSEL.**

93

What is a belt with a watch on it called?

• **A WAIST of time.**

94

When told "You are a werewolf,"

• **The werewolf responds, "I am aware."**

95

Why was the cookie so sad?

• **Because his dad was a WAFER so long.**

96

I went to the store and picked up eight cans of soda,

• **but when I left I realized I only picked 7-UP.**

97

What do cows tell each other before bedtime?

• **Dairy tales.**

98

What is orange but sounds like a parrot?

- **A CARROT.**

99

When Halloween comes around,

- **October is nearly Octover.**

100

What do you say when you get beat at a barbeque race?

- **I relish the fact that you mustard the strength to ketchup to me.**

101

When the aquatic mammals at the zoo escaped,

- **things were OTTER chaos.**

102

What do drummers name their daughters?

- **Anna one, Anna two!**

103

Is your fridge currently running?
- **Because I need someone to vote for.**

104

I ordered a book of dad jokes last week,
- **but I didn't GET it.**

105

Do you want to hear a joke about construction?
- **It's not ready yet, still WORKING on it.**

106

Five out of four people admit that they can't understand fractions.

107

Why do cookies visit the doctor often?
- **Because they always feel CRUMMY.**

108

Last night I dreamed that I was drowning in a sea of orange soda.

- **I finally realized that it was just a FANTA-SEA when I woke up.**

109

How was your camping trip?

- **It was in TENTS.**

110

I decided to give all my batteries away today,

- **free of charge.**

111

What did the child who refused to sleep during nap time really do?

- **He resisted arrest.**

112

What kind of cars do sheep drive?

- **SuBAAArus.**

113

My friends like to say that I'm the cheapest person in the world,

- **but I don't buy it.**

114

What has four wheels and flies?

- **A garbage truck.**

115

What is the main difference between a guy dressed in pajamas on a tricycle and a guy dressed in a suit on a bicycle?

- **AtTIRE.**

116

Don't you hate it when people answer their OWN questions?

- **Because I do.**

117

Did you hear about those two men who stole a calendar?

- **Each of them got six months.**

118

Recently, I bumped into the man who sold me an antique globe at the store.

- It's such a **SMALL WORLD.**

119

What kind of shoes do spies wear?

- **SNEAKers.**

120

A horse walks into a restaurant. The waiter asks him,

- **"Why the long face?"**

121

Is rivalry between two vegetarians called a BEEF or something else?

122

Why do pirates always fail to finish the alphabet?

- **Because they get lost at C!**

32

123

Why do trees always have so many friends?

• **Because they know how to BRANCH OUT!**

124

I have a lot of my dad's genes. Really?

• **I bet they don't fit!**

125

What is it called when an apple is thrown at your face?

• **A fruit punch.**

126

How did the flashlight feel when his power died?

• **He was deLIGHTED.**

127

What confuses ants the most?

• **The fact that all of his uncles are ants.**

128 What did Santa Claus say to Mrs. Claus when he looked up at the sky?

- **Looks like rain, dear!**

129 What method of coffee making does Moses use?

- **He BREWS it.**

130 The way people are making apocalypse jokes,

- **it's like there is no tomorrow!**

131 Why did my friends wear sunglasses when I entered the classroom?

- **Because I am such a bright student.**

132 What do you call it when birds stick close together?

- **VelCROWS.**

133

What similarity do baseball teams and pancakes share?

- **They both need good batters to succeed.**

134

What do vegetables say at parties?

- **Lettuce turnip the beet!**

135

What is a tornado's favorite board game?

- **TWISTER.**

136

What do eggs do on the weekends for fun?

- **Kara-yolkie.**

137

What is it called when your sister is crying?

- **A criSIS.**

138

Why can't pirates play card games?

- **Because they're always sitting on top of the DECK.**

139

Why did the baker stop making doughnuts and bagels?

- **Because he got tired of the HOLE thing.**

140

Why did the coach have to kick Cinderella off of the softball team?

- **Because she kept running away from the ball.**

141

Why was the King only twelve inches tall?

- **Because he was the RULER.**

142

What is the most slippery country in the world?

- **Greece.**

143 Why was the skeleton so afraid of crossing the street?
- **Because he didn't have the guts.**

144 Why do some cell phones wear glasses?
- **Because they lost their contacts.**

145 Why shouldn't you trust trees?
- **Because they are shady.**

146 Why can't suntanning be an Olympic sport?
- **Because the best award you can ever get is bronze.**

147 What will happen if you eat yeast and polish for breakfast every morning?
- **You will rise and shine!**

148 I'm considering going on an all-almond diet,
- **but that's NUTS!**

149 Is your refrigerator running?
- **You better go catch it!**

150 What genre of music scares balloons?
- **Pop music.**

151 Have you heard about that new restaurant on the moon?
- **The food is pretty great, but there's no atmosphere!!**

152 What did the plate say to the plate beside it?
- **Lunch is ON me.**

38

153

I may get a haircut,
- **but first I should MULLET over.**

154

You know, some days are stronger than others. Saturdays and Sundays especially,
- **since the rest are weekdays.**

155

This guy was hit in the head with a bottle of Sprite.
- **But he's okay because it was a SOFT drink.**

156

Are you cold?
- **Go stand in the corner; it's 90 degrees.**

157

What do alligators have to drink when they're feeling thirsty?
- **GATORade.**

158

Have you heard about the man who died after falling into a machine at the glasses factory?

• **He really made a SPECTACLE of himself.**

159

What does Earth constantly tell the other planets?

• **To get a life!**

160

Why do golfers like to wear not one, but two pairs of pants?

• **In case they get a HOLE in one!**

161

What did Snow White say when she exited the photo booth?

• **One day, my PRINTS will come...**

162

Where do acrobatic waiters work?

• **IHOP!**

163

What did the evil chicken lay?

- **Deviled eggs.**

164

Have you heard about the three holes in the ground filled to the brims with water? No?

- **Well, well, well...**

165

What did the daddy chimney say to the young chimney?

- **You're far too young to start smoking.**

166

If anyone needs an ark,

- **I happen to Noah guy.**

167

What is a guy with a rubber toe called?

- **Rober-to!**

168

What is a cow with no legs called?

- **Ground beef.**

169

What do runners eat before running a race?

- **Nothing, because they fast.**

170

Which bones do dogs avoid eating?

- **Trombones.**

171

Because when he asked them who they thought the best musical composer was, they'd all shout,

- **"Bach, bach, bach!!"**

172

Why do sea-gulls fly over the sea?

- **Because if they fly over a bay, they will be called "Bagels."**

173

What lies at the bottom of the ocean and shakes?

• **A nervous WRECK.**

174

What happened when the cow tried jumping through a barbed-wire fence?

• **UTTER destruction.**

175

What has four legs, is fuzzy and green, and if it fell from the sky it would kill you?

• **A pool table!**

176

What's the difference between having the swine flu and having the bird flu?

• **If you have the swine flu, you need oinkment, while if you have the bird flu you need tweetment.**

177

Why do ghosts love to ride in elevators so much?

• **Because elevators lift their spirits.**

178

How do snails argue?

• **They slug it out!**

179

What kind of person can shave 25 times a day but still have a beard?

• **A barber.**

180

What happened to the excited gardener when spring arrived?

• **He wet his PLANTS.**

181

Have you heard about those two peanuts that were walking through Central Park?

• **One was a-SALTED.**

182

When there is no more coffee left, how do you feel?

• **Depresso.**

183

What do frogs like to drink?

• **Croacka Cola.**

184

What do you call it when you throw your boomerang and it doesn't return?

• **A stick.**

185

What is a line of backward-marching rabbits called?

• **A receding hairline.**

186

What is a pony with a sore throat called?

• **A little horse.**

187

What will happen if a frog parks illegally?

- **It will get Toad.**

188

What do you give a lemon who is sick?

- **Lemon-AID.**

189

Which musical instrument can be found in the bathroom?

- **A tuba toothpaste!**

190

Whatever you do, don't trust atoms.

- **They make up everything.**

191

I only know 25 letters out of 26 in the alphabet.

- **I don't know WHY.**

192

What do you call a cheese that's always lonely?

- **A provoLONE.**

193

What does a pepper do when it is angry?

- **It gets jalapeno in your face!**

194

What is a person without a body or a nose called?

- **Nobody knows.**

195

What did the traffic light say to the crosswalk when it changed colors?

- **Don't look at me right now, I'm changing!"**

196

I can't tell if I like my new blender yet,

- **I have MIXED feelings.**

197
Did you hear that the giant threw up?
• **It's all over town.**

198
What is a fly without wings called?
• **A walk!**

199
Why do bees make humming noises?
• **Because they cannot speak.**

200
Without geometry,
• **there is no POINT to life.**

201
Why is it so hard to listen while a pterodactyl goes to the bathroom?
• **Because the pee is completely silent.**

202

What is a deer with no eyes called?

- **No eye-deer.**

203

Why was the cat asked to quit the running race?

- **Because it was a CHEETAH.**

204

When is it time to go visit the dentist?

- **Tooth-hurty.**

205

Why is the word "dark" spelled with a k instead of a c?

- **Because you can't C in the dark.**

206

What's the difference between me and a calendar?

- **A calendar can get dates, and I can't.**

207

Where does an army general keep his armies?

• **In his SLEEVies.**

208

What did the hat say to the rack of hats?

• **"You stay here, I'm gonna go on ahead."**

209

Why couldn't the mushroom host his birthday party?

• **Because there wasn't MUCH room.**

210

Why did the broom arrive so late to work?

• **It overSWEPT.**

211

When my son told me, "Stop impersonating a flamingo,"

• **I really had to put my foot down.**

212

I was up all night wondering where the sun had gone

- **when it dawned on me.**

213

Once you've seen one shopping place,

- **you've seen them-ALL.**

214

My dolphin puns are terrible,

- **but at least I do it on porpoise.**

215

I've been thinking of reasons to go to Switzerland.

- **The flag is a big plus.**

216

Time flies like a plane.

- **Fruit flies like a banana.**

217

Why did some tomatoes blush before being tossed in a salad?

- **Because they saw the salad DRESSING.**

218

What happened to the magic tractor?

- **It turned straight into a field.**

219

Why must bananas wear sunscreen?

- **Because they peel.**

220

What do you call a can that eats other cans?

- **A CANnibal.**

221

What does a house wear?

- **A-DRESS.**

222

I quit my job at the coffee shop
- **Because it was the same GRIND every day.**

223

Do you want to hear a word that I just came up with?
- **Plagiarism.**

224

I used to work at the calendar factory,
- **but I was fired for taking too many days off.**

225

Rest in peace, boiled water.
- **You will be mist.**

226

What did zero say to eight?
- **"I like your belt, eight!"**

227

How can you tell that a vampire has a cold?
- **They start coffin!**

228

What is a vampire's favorite fruit to snack on?
- **A blood-orange.**

229

What is a funny mountain called?
- **Hill-arious.**

230

Where do baby cows go for lunch?
- **The calf-ateria.**

231

What is a room that nobody can go into?
- **A MUSHroom.**

232

What did the father buffalo tell his son when he drove to school?

• **BiSON.**

233

What is a dysfunctional can opener called?

• **A can't-opener.**

234

Why do eye doctors live for such a long time?

• **They diLATE.**

235

I wouldn't buy anything that had velcro on it.

• **It's a total RIP-off.**

236

What do spiders wear to weddings?

• **A webbing dress.**

237

What do you call an elf with a lot of money?

• **Welfy.**

238

What do birds give out to their neighbors on Halloween?

• **Tweets.**

239

What do you call a group of trees who are really smart?

• **A brain-forest.**

240

I would tell a joke about time travel,

• **but you guys didn't like it before.**

241

What is a fake noodle called?

• **An impasta.**

242

How do you get a squirrel to like you?
- **You gotta act like a nut.**

243

Why don't eggs tell jokes?
- **Because they'd crack each other up.**

244

I don't trust stairs... you know,
- **they're always up to something.**

245

Did you hear the rumor about butter?
- **Well, I'm certainly not going to spread it around.**

246

Why couldn't the bicycle get through the day?
- **It was two-tired.**

247

How do you make a tissue dance around?

- **You gotta put a little boogie inside of it.**

248

What is it called when you have cheese that doesn't belong to you?

- **Nacho cheese.**

249

What do oceans do to communicate?

- **They wave!**

250

Is hot or cold faster?

- **Hot, because you can catch a cold!**

251

Why do leopards have so much trouble hiding?

- **Because they are always spotted.**

252

What is an alligator wearing a vest called?

- **An investigator.**

253

What is brown and sticky all around?

- **A stick!**

254

Why did the invisible guy turn down the job that he was offered?

- **He just couldn't see himself doing the job.**

255

How do trees access the internet?

- **They log on!**

256

What do eyes say to each other?

- **Between you and me, something smells.**

257

When a cow is stuck in an earthquake, what is she called?

• **A milkshake.**

258

Why is the doctor so calm?

• **Because she has a lot of patients.**

259

What do astronomers do before a party?

• **They planet.**

260

Why is Peter Pan always in the sky?

• **Because he neverlands.**

261

Two guys walked into a bar.

• **The third one ducked under.**

262

Why is bees' hair so sticky all the time?

- **Because they brush it with a honeycomb.**

263

Did you hear about that kidnapping today?

- **Well, don't worry, he woke up eventually.**

264

Why couldn't the crab share with his friends?

- **Because he was shellfish.**

265

Where does someone learn to make ice cream?

- **Sundae school.**

266

Which word is spelled wrong in the dictionary?

- **The word "wrong."**

267

What did the baby corn say to the mom corn?

- **Where is my popcorn?**

268

Why did the football coach go to the bank?

- **To retrieve his quarterback.**

269

Where do pencils go on vacation?

- **Pencil-vania.**

270

What is a rabbit's favorite way to dance?

- **Hip-HOP!**

271

What do lawyers wear to work?

- **LawSUITS.**

272
What texture of hair do oceans have?
• WAVY.

273
What do you call a bear without teeth?
• A gummy bear.

274
How do you communicate with a giant?
• You use BIG words.

275
What does a lion say to other animals when he meets them?
• Pleased to EAT you.

276
Did you hear about the cheese factory explosion in France?
• All that was left was de Brie.

277

What do you get from a cow who was given everything he wanted growing up?

• **Spoiled milk.**

278

What is a cat's absolute favorite color?

• **Purrrrrrple.**

279

How many apples grow on a tree?

• **All of the apples.**

280

This graveyard looks super crowded.

• **Everyone must be DYING to get in here.**

281

What did the mommy spider say to the kid spider?

• **You're spending too much time on the web.**

282

What is a dad's all-time favorite dinosaur?

• **A dad-asaurus!**

283

What did the grape do when someone crushed it?

• **He let out a little wine!**

284

I'm reading a book about the history of glue,

• **and I can't seem to put it down.**

285

Is this pool safe to dive in?

• **It deep-ends.**

286

What does a slow tomato say to the other tomatoes?

• **"Don't worry, I will ketchup.**

287

Why did the scarecrow get so much praise?

- **Because he is outstanding in his field.**

288

What does one call a dinosaur who is sleeping?

- **A dino-SNORE!**

289

How does Darth Vader take his toast?

- **On the dark side.**

290

How do celebrities stay cool?

- **They have tons of fans surrounding them all the time.**

291

My wife always has trouble unbuckling our daughter's car seat with one hand, so she asked me, "How do one-armed mothers do it?" I replied,

- **"Single-handedly..."**

292

I would tell you a joke about pizza,

- **but it's a bit cheesy.**

293

Does February March?

- **No, but April May!**

294

What sound does the engine of a witch's car make?

- **Broom, broom.**

295
What's that city in Nevada where all the dentists go?
- **Oh right, Floss Vegas.**

296
Why don't skeletons like to go trick or treating on Halloween?
- **They have no body to accompany them.**

297
I was wondering why this frisbee kept getting bigger and bigger.
- **Then it hit me right in the face.**

298
I was going to share a vegetable joke,
- **but it may be kind of corny.**

299
What is the loudest pet you can get?
- **A trumPET.**

300

What kind of tea should you drink when you visit the Queen?

- **RoyalTEA.**

301

What is a dog with magical abilities called?

- **A Labracadabrador.**

302

When do ducks wake up in the morning?

- **At the quack of dawn.**

303

Why did the girl smear peanut butter on the road?

- **It goes nicely with traffic jams!**

304

Why did the child cross the playground?

- **To reach the other slide.**

305

Want me to tell you a joke about paper?

- **Never mind, it's really tear-able!**

306

I am guilty...

- **Of making courthouse puns.**

307

Time flies,

- **even if turkeys don't.**

308

There are two muffins cooking in the oven. One says, "It's hot in here," and the other says,

- **"Oh my gosh! This muffin is talking to me!"**

CHAPTER 2
HYPER-LITERAL JOKES

01

Dad, can you put the cat out?

- **Sure, but I didn't know it was on FIRE.**

02

I'd like to give a big shout out to all the sidewalks out there,

- **who keep me off the streets safe and sound.**

03

What happens once every minute, twice in a moment, and never in a decade?

- **The letter "M."**

04

Never judge someone until you have walked a mile in their shoes.

- **That way, when you do judge them, you will be a mile away and you'll have their shoes.**

05

Man: Are you the person who sold me this tube yesterday, telling me that it was toothpaste?

Cashier: Yes indeed!

- **Man: Well, I tried it over and over again this morning, but my teeth still won't stay stuck in my mouth.**

06

Son: Dad, someone is at the door collecting donations for a community swimming pool.

- **Dad: Okay, just give him a glass of water.**

07

Where was the constitution of England signed?

- **At the bottom of the page, of course!**

08

Last night, my friends and I watched three movies, all in a row.

- **Thankfully, I was the one who got to face the TV.**

09

I accidentally spilled some rice in my headphones,

- **so now all of my music sounds GRAINY.**

10

If the right side of the brain is the one to control the left side of the human body,

- **then I suppose left-handed people are the only ones in their right mind.**

11

Where were you born?
The United States.
Which part?

- **All my body parts.**

12

Don't ever break anyone's heart; they only have one.

- **Instead, break their bones. They have 206 of them.**

13

If number two pencils are so loved,

- **then why are they still ranked number two?**

14

What can you give and keep all at once?

- **A common cold.**

15

Science teacher: What is the chemical formula for water?

Student: HIJKLMNO

Science teacher: Where did you get that from??

- **Student: You said yesterday that the chemical formula for water was H to O.**

16

I went to the doctor because I broke my arm in two different places, and the doctor replied,

- **"Stay out of those two places, would ya?"**

17

When my boss said, "Have a good day,"

- **I just went home.**

18

Why can't someone have a twelve-inch long nose?

- **Because then it wouldn't be a nose; it would be a foot.**

19

Why do birds fly to the South for the winter?

- **Because it's too far of a walk.**

20

I love telling Dad jokes because sometimes,

- **he laughs!**

21

Dad, can you put my shoes on?

- **No, of course not! They would never fit me.**

22

If someone says, "I'll call you later," say,

- **"Don't call me that; call me Dad."**

23

I wonder if a kangaroo can jump higher than a house...

- **Of course, because a house can't jump!**

24

Did you get a haircut?

- **No, I cut every single one.**

25

Did you brush your teeth?
- **No, only a couple of them.**

26

I'm such a sleeping pro
- **That I can do it with my EYES closed.**

27

What are the world's most intelligent animals?
- **Fish. They stay in schools.**

28

What's the name of the guy who always lies on our doorstep?
- **Oh yeah, Matt.**

29

Dad, can you make me pancakes?

- **Sure! Poof — you are now pancakes.**

30

I just fell off of a fifty-foot ladder!

Oh my, are you okay?

- **Yeah, I'm good. I only fell off of the first step of the ladder.**

31

What is the tallest building in a city?

- **The library. It has so many stories.**

32

How do you know that there is an elephant under your bed?

- **Your head hits the ceiling.**

33

Guess who I ran into on my way to get my eyeglasses fixed?

- **Pretty much everyone.**

34

Due to quarantine, from now on,

- **it's all INSIDE jokes from me.**

35

What is brown and not too heavy?

- **LIGHT brown.**

36

What color of paint is blue but smells like it's red paint?

- **Blue paint.**

37

Did you hear about that woman who dreamed that she was eating a marshmallow?

- **She woke up, and her pillow had completely disappeared.**

38

What is the least SPOKEN language ever?

- **Sign language.**

39

A sandwich orders a drink at the cafe. The waiter replies,

- **"Sorry we don't serve food here."**

40

The cashier said, "Would you like the milk bagged sir?" so Dad said,

- **"No, I prefer my milk in cartons."**

41

If someone asks you if you are alright, say,

• **"No, I am half left."**

42

If someone asks you, "How do I look?" say,

• **"With your eyes."**

43

If someone asks, "Blood type?" say,

• **"Red!"**

44

Why couldn't someone make a reservation at the library?

• **Because they were all BOOKED.**

45

If someone says, "Well," say,

- **"That's a DEEP subject."**

46

I am scared for the calendar.

- **Its days are numbered!**

47

Yesterday, I accidentally ate a bit of food coloring. The doctor says I'll be fine,

- **but I feel like I've DYED inside.**

48

If your kid says, "Can I watch TV?" say,

- **"Yes, but don't turn it on."**

49

I am reading a book all about gravity,

- **and it's impossible to put down.**

50

What rhymes with orange?

- **No, it doesn't.**

51

If your kid says, "I think I got a sunburn," say,

- **"No, I think you got a daughter burn."**

52

To the person who invented the number zero,

- **thanks a lot for nothing.**

5 3

I told my friend that I hate my haircut,
to which they responded,

- **"It will grow on you."**

5 4

Why is math so sad?

- **Because it has so many problems.**

5 5

How come there are so many Johnsons in the
phone book?

- **Because they all have phones, I guess.**

01

Someone walks into a bookstore and says to the cashier, "Can I have a book by Shakespeare?" He replies, "Of course, but which one?"

- **The man says, "William, of course."**

02

Dave: I made a huge mistake today by giving my dad soap flakes instead of Corn Flakes for breakfast.

Lily: Was he mad at you for it?

- **Dave: Yeah, he was FOAMING at the mouth.**

03

For a while, the magician Houdini was using a trap door in every show that he did.

- **I suppose you could say he was going through a STAGE.**

04

Why did the coffee go to the police station to file a report?

- **Because it got MUGged.**

05

Father: Let me see your report card.

Son: I don't have it, sorry.

Father: Where is it?

- **Son: My friend has it. He wants to scare his parents.**

06

Dad: How are you liking fourth grade?

Son: It isn't great, honestly.

- **Dad: Oh yeah? It was the best four years of my life!**

07

Dad: How much money do you need?

Son: I'll be good for 20.

- **Dad: When I was your age, I was good for nothing.**

08

When my daughter yelled, "Daaad, have you listened to one word I've said?" I replied,

- **"What a rude way to START a conversation with me!"**

09

A man sued the airline company because he lost his luggage.

- **Unfortunately, he lost his CASE.**

10

A family is at the zoo, looking at the ferocious tigers. The kid asks the parents, "If the tigers made it out of the cage and ate you both..." The parents replied, "Aw, sweetie, don't worry," and the kid said,

- **"...then which bus would I need to take home?"**

11

After paying for his hotdog, the Buddhist asked the cashier, "Where is my change?" The cashier replied,

- **"Change must come from within you."**

12

When I met some aliens from outer space,

- **I thought they were pretty down to Earth.**

13

I really shouldn't have had the seafood for dinner.

- **I'm feeling a little eel.**

14

My wife can be so negative sometimes. I remembered to bring the car seat, the diaper bag, and the carriage.

- **But all she can focus on is the fact that I forgot the BABY.**

15

John: What does your dad do for a living?

Kevin: He is a magician.

John: Do you have any siblings?

- **Kevin: Yes, four half-sisters, and a half-brother. My dad needs someone to practice on.**

16

Two satellites got married. The wedding was alright,

- **but the RECEPTION was breathtaking.**

17

Tim: How do you like the drum set that you got for Christmas?

Nina: I love it, but I try not to use it much!

Tim: How come?

- **Nina: My mom gives me ten bucks every time I don't play it.**

18

"I'll take a Coke," said the man.

"Do you want that in a can?" said the flight attendant.

- **"No, I'll drink it right here, thank you."**

19

Before you go into the bathroom, you are American, and after you exit the bathroom, you are American, but what are you while you are inside of the bathroom?

- **European.**

20

Dad: What is the difference between a pack of water bottles and a pack of wolves?

Son: I don't know. Tell me!

- **Dad: I don't know the answer either, so it's a good thing that Mom does the grocery shopping around here.**

21

At first, I could hardly believe that my dad had stolen from his road-working job.

- **But when I went by his place, all of the signs were there.**

22

Two cannibals are eating a clown for breakfast. One of the cannibals says to the other,

- **"Does this taste FUNNY to you?"**

23

Jessica: When does a joke become a dad joke?

Lincoln: I don't know!

- **Jessica: When it becomes apPARENT.**

24

Dad: If you keep yanking on my hair, you're gonna have to get off my shoulders and walk beside me.

- **Son: But Dad, I'm just trying to get the gum that I lost back!**

25

Teacher on the phone: So you're saying that Jason has a cold and can't make it to school today. To whom am I speaking?

- **Jason: This is my father.**

26

Son: Dad, is it good to eat bugs?

Father: Let's not talk about gross things at the dinner table, son.

(After dinner)

Father: Son, what did you want to ask me?

- **Son: Oh, never mind. There was a bug in your soup, but that's in the past now.**

Science teacher: When do you reach the boiling point?

- **Science student: When my mom sees my report card!**

28

Four men are sitting in the hospital waiting room because their wives are giving birth. A nurse approaches the first man and says, "Congrats, you're the father of twins!"

The man responds, "How funny, I work for the Minnesota Twins!"

The nurse approaches the second man and says, "Congratulations, you're the father of triplets!"

The man responds, "How funny, I work for the 3M company!"

The nurse approaches the third man and says, "Congratulations, you're the father of quadruplets!"

The man responds, "How funny, I work for the Four Seasons Hotel!"

Another man starts groaning and clutching his head in his lap. "What's wrong?" the other three men inquire.

- **The fourth man replies, "I work for 7-Up!"**

29

A waiter serves a woman a cup of coffee. The woman takes her first sip and spits it right out. She turns to the waiter and says, "This coffee tastes an awful lot like mud." The waiter, looking shocked, says

- **"But, ma'am, it's fresh GROUND!"**

30

A kid stumbles upon a magical lamp. He starts rubbing the lamp, and a genie appears to ask the kid what his first wish is. The kid wishes that he were rich. The genie says,

- **"It's done! What is your second wish, Rich?"**

31

Three best friends are stranded on a deserted island, and they find a magic lamp. The genie inside the lamp offers to grant each friend one wish, for a total of three wishes. The first friend wishes, "I want to go home." The second friend wishes, "I want to go home, too." The third friend says,

- **"I'm lonely. I sure wish my friends were back here."**

32

A guy asks his friend to go to the dance with him. She says yes, so he decides to rent a suit. The rental place has a long line, so the guy waits and waits until he finally can get his suit.

He decides that he should buy flowers for his friend, so he goes to the florist.

There is a long line in the flower shop, so he waits and waits until he finally can get his bouquet of flowers.

The guy arrives at his friend's house and they go to the dance. There is a long line outside of the school, so they wait and wait. Finally, when they arrive inside the school, the guy offers to go get his friend a drink.

- **At the drink table, there is no punch line.**

33

At the grocery store, a customer drops a big bag of flour. A boy scout runs to help the guy, picking it up for him.

- **"Don't worry, young man. It's self-rising," said the customer.**

34

A woman walks into the library and approaches the circulation desk. "I'll have a cheeseburger, fries, a Coca-Cola, and actually, make that double!" The librarian replies, "Do you know that this is a library, ma'am?" to which the woman says,

- "Sorry," whispering, "I'll have two cheeseburgers, fries, and a Coca-Cola."

35

A man was driving down the highway when he was stopped by a police officer who was following him. The officer discovered a pile of penguins when he examined a suspicious lump in the back of the man's pickup truck.

"Sir, why are there penguins in your truck?"

The man said, "Because these are my penguins. They belong to me."

The officer said, "You need to take them to the zoo."

The next day, the officer saw the same man, with the same lump, and pulled him over. After examining the back of the truck, the policeman discovered that the penguins were wearing sunglasses.

"I thought I was clear when I told you to take these penguins to the zoo," the officer said.

- "I did," the man said. "And today is beach day!"

36

One time, there was a prince who was put under a spell that he could only speak one word each year. If the prince skipped a year, he could save up that word and speak double the amount the next year.

One day, the prince fell in love with a beautiful woman. He wanted so badly to call her "My darling," so he avoided speaking for two years. Then, he wanted to tell her, "I love you," so he avoided speaking for three years. At the end of this five-year journey, he wanted to propose to her, so he waited for another four years.

Once the ninth year of silence had ended, he took this woman to a beautiful part of the kingdom and said, "I love you. Will you marry me?"

- **The woman replied, "Pardon me?"**

37

One day, a boy read a sign in the shop window that said it sold "fat-free" french fries. Being health-conscious, the boy ordered some fries. He watched the cook make the fries, potatoes dripping with oil and all. The boy said, "Wait a minute, chef. These do not look fat-free." The chef said,

- **"Sure they are! We only charge for the potatoes, not the fat. So, the fat is free!"**

38

Three men are in the middle of the desert when their car breaks down. They have to hike to town, so they each decide to bring only one thing with them. One man brings with him a jug of water. Another man brings with him a sandwich. The third man removes one of the car doors and starts walking.

The first man says, "I'm bringing water because if I get thirsty, I can drink it. And it makes sense to bring a sandwich because if we get hungry, we can eat it. But why do you have with you a car door?"

- **The last man says, "If I get hot, I can roll down the window!"**

39

One day, a man with a pet elephant walked into the theater to see a movie.

"I'm sorry sir, but your elephant cannot accompany you to the movie. He isn't allowed in the building," the manager said.

"Oh, I can promise you, sir, he is well-behaved, better than most people are," the man said.

"Okay, then. If you're sure…"

After the movie ended, the manager said to the man, "I'm surprised to say the least. Your elephant was well-behaved, and he seemed to really enjoy the movie!"

- **"I was surprised too. He hated the book!"**

40

Joe visited his 90-year-old grandfather who lives out in the countryside. On the first morning of the visit, Joe's grandpa made them a beautiful breakfast of bacon and eggs. Joe noticed a weird, film-like substance on his plate. "Grandpa, these plates are clean, right?"

Joe's grandpa replied, "They're as clean as hot water can get them. Just don't worry, and finish your meal."

For lunch, grandpa prepared a beautiful lunch of hamburgers, salads, and vegetables. John noticed the same film on his plate, in addition to some dried up eggs, probably from this morning's breakfast. "Are you sure these plates are clean, grandpa??" Joe asked.

Without looking up, grandpa said, "I said it before, and I'll say it again. Those dishes are clean as hot water can get them."

As Joe was leaving later, his grandpa's dog growled and wouldn't let Joe exit. Joe said, "Grandpa, your dog won't let me get through!"

- **Joe's grandpa yelled at the dog, "Hot Water, go lie down, won't ya??"**

41

A guy goes door to door looking for a job. One homeowner hands him a brush and a can of paint, offering him 150 dollars to paint his porch.

A few hours later, the man returns and says to the homeowner,

- **"I'm done, but you should know that your car is a Ferrari, not a Porsche."**

42

A cruise ship passes an island that is in the middle of nowhere, and all the passengers see a bearded man running around and flailing his arms around.

"Captain, who is that man over there?"

- **The captain says, "I have no clue, but every year he makes a fuss like this when we pass him by."**

43

A guy named Jerry is sitting at home when he hears a knocking sound at his front door. He opens the door to find a snail, sitting on the stoop. He picks up the snail and chucks it as far away from himself as possible. One year later, there is another knocking sound at the man's front door. He opens it to find the same exact snail. The snail says,

- **"What was all that about, dude??"**

44

My friend thinks he is smart. When he told me that onions are the only food that can make you cry,

- **I threw a coconut at him to prove him wrong. It worked.**

45

Math teacher: If I gave you two cats and another four cats, how many cats would you have?

Sydney: Seven.

Math teacher: No, listen more closely. If I gave you two cats and another four cats, how many cats would you have?

Sydney: Still seven.

Math teacher: Let me phrase this a different way. If I gave you two apples and another four apples, how many apples would you have?

Sydney: Six apples.

Math teacher: Good. Now, what does that look like but with cats?

Sydney: Seven.

Math teacher: Sydney, how are you getting seven in your calculations?

- **Sydney: I already have a cat at home.**

46

One day, two brothers played a game of hide and go seek. One brother was named Mind Your Own Business, and the other was named Trouble. Trouble hid, while Mind Your Own Business tried to find him. Mind Your Own Business started to search for his brother under cars and behind bushes. A police officer approached him and said, "What is your name?" The boy replied, "Mind your own business." The policeman, angry, asked, "Are you looking for trouble, kid?" The boy replied,

- **"Yes, how'd you know?!"**

47

A teacher challenges her students to include the word "beans" in a sentence to practice learning its definition. One girl says, "My father grows beans," and another student says, "I like to cook beans in my burritos." The third student says,

- **"We are all human beans."**

48

The math teacher says, "If I have five bottles in one hand and six in the other hand, what do I have?"

- **The student replies, "a very thirsty teacher."**

49

An elderly couple started to notice that they were getting more and more forgetful, so they decided to visit a doctor. The doctor said to them that they should start writing themselves reminders to avoid forgetting everything.

After the appointment, they headed home and the old lady told her husband to get a bowl of ice cream. "You should write that down, dear," she said to him. The husband replied, "No, I can remember that." She urged him to write it down over and over again. The husband refused and proceeded to go into the kitchen to get her the ice cream.

He spent an unusual amount of time in the kitchen, almost 30 minutes. Finally, he exited the kitchen and gave his wife a plate of eggs and bacon. The wife stared at the plate in awe, eventually saying,

- **"Where is the toast?"**

50

One time, I went to the 24-hour grocery store because it was late at night, and nowhere else was open. The guy was locking the front door when I arrived. I said, "Hey! The sign says you are open 24/7, so why are you closing shop?" The man said,

- **"Yes, we are open 24 hours, but not in a row, silly!"**

51

A man called his child's doctor because his son swallowed the pen that he was writing with. "What should I do?" the man pleaded. The doctor advised,

- **"Until I come over, just write with another pen."**

52

John, Sal, and Alice are tired after traveling all day and night, so they check into a hotel. At the reception desk, they discover that they'll have to walk about 75 flights of stairs to get to their room since the elevator is not operating.

John recommends that they do something fun to pass the time while they walk the flights. John will tell jokes, Sal will sing songs, and Alice will tell scary stories. John tells jokes for 25 of the flights, Sal sings songs for the 25 other flights, and Alice tells scary stories for 24. When they reach the last floor, Alice tells her scariest story of all,

- **"Guys, I, unfortunately, left the room key at reception."**

53

Two lawyers walking through the woods spot a gruesome bear. The first lawyer opens his briefcase, pulls out a pair of sneakers and starts lacing them up. The second lawyer says, "You're insane if you think you can outrun that bear." The first lawyer responds,

- **"I don't have to outrun him, I only have to outrun you!"**

54

A man sees a sign on someone's home that says, "Talking dog for sale." The man walks into the house to inquire about the offer. "What have you done with your life so far?" he asks the talking dog. The dog replies, "I've led a full life. I lived in the mountains rescuing victims of avalanches, then served in the war. Now I spend my time reading to elderly people in a community home." The man was shocked. He asked the talking dog's owner, "Why would you ever get rid of an amazing dog like that?" The owner said,

- **"Because he has a lying problem. He never did any of that stuff!"**

Book

Book

Book

55

A chicken marches into the library and walks up to the circulation desk, shouting, "Book, book, BOOK!"

The librarian hands him a couple of small children's books and watches the chicken as it exits the library. The chicken walks across the street and through a field, disappearing down a hill right afterward.

The next day, the chicken returns to the library. He walks right up to the desk, drops the book on it, and says, "BOOK, BOOK!"

The librarian hands him a few more books and watches him drag the books away from the desk.

Once the chicken has left, the librarian follows him through the field and down the hill, where there lies a small pond. On a rock at the edge of the pond is a huge frog, the biggest one that the librarian has ever seen. The chicken walks up to the frog, drops the book on the edge of the pond, and says "Book, book, book!"

The frog hops over it, pushing through the large stack of books, and says

- **"Read it, read it, read it!"**

56

Teacher: "Kyle, where is your homework?"

Kyle: "My dog ate it."

Teacher: "Kyle, I have been a teacher for almost twenty years. Do you really think I'm going to believe that?"

- **Kyle: "It's true, I swear. I covered it with peanut butter and he scarfed it down."**

57

A bus driver sees a stranded van from the zoo on the side of the road, and he wants to help. When he pulls over, the zoo van driver offers the bus driver 100 dollars to help him deliver the dozens of penguins in the back. The driver agrees, and he does the job.

About two hours later, the zoo worker fixes his van and heads back to the zoo. He sees the bus driver driving in the wrong direction when he gets back on the road and yells, "Why are you still driving the penguins around? I asked you to take them back to the zoo, where they belong."

- **The bus driver said to him, "Calm down. I did take them to the zoo. But they were bored, so we're heading back to my place for a barbeque. You're welcome to join!"**

FINAL WORDS

First off, thanks for taking the time to read my book!

I hope you got as many laughs from reading it as I did from writing it – which was honestly quite a lot.

But I should note that you are not done yet.

See, the best thing about this big book of dad jokes is that they do not expire. Yep, you can share them over and over again with your friends and family *whenever* you want.

So, what are you waiting for? Go ahead and make your friends and family giggle – because honestly, nothing would make me happier.